The Tarnation of Faust

The Tarnation of Faust

POEMS

David Case

Gunpowder Press • Santa Barbara
2014

© 2014 by the Estate of David Allen Case

Published by Gunpowder Press
David Starkey, Editor
PO Box 60035
Santa Barbara, CA 93160-0035

Front cover photo: Ed Lazzara
Back cover photo: Gary Kirkland

ISBN-13: 978-0-9916651-0-5

www.gunpowderpress.com

Acknowledgements:
Electronic Poetry Review: "The Tarnation of Faust," "Couldn't Let Go of L.A.," "The Spleen of Ocean Avenue."
In a Fine Frenzy: Poets Respond to Shakespeare, edited by David Starkey and Paul J. Willis (Iowa, 2005): "Fear No More."
The Southern Review: "Palms at Christmas."

For Carolie Parker, David Starkey and Katherine Anne Swiggart,
sustainers of the universe

CONTENTS

PLAYING DEBUSSY IN THE HEART OF DIXIE

Picture Poem   12
History of the Early Seventies I   13
History of the Early Seventies II   14
History of the Early Seventies III   15
Funky Town, First Week of College   16
Wild Horses   17
East Jesus   19
Smack-Down   21
Grief-Skin   22
Metronome   23
Back Home   24

PALMS AT CHRISTMAS

South   26
Couldn't Let Go of L.A.   28
"Me llamo Bond ... Jaime Bond"   29
Spleen of Ocean Avenue   30
The Great Williams   31
You Don't Know What Love Is   32
Palms at Christmas   34
Auld Lang Syne   35
Fear No More   36
From the Center of the Universe   37
Jesus of San Gabriel   38
Just What I Needed   39
Sounds and Aromas Revolving in Evening Air   40
Mass Transit   41

PAVILLON DES MALADIES MORTELLES

Canal St. Martin   44
Epistemology of Vanished Currencies   45
As the World Turns   47
D---------   48
Swing   50
A Dream of Absolution   51
An American in Paris   52
Monet by Renoir   53
Pavilion des maladies mortelles   54

DERRIDA, REMBRANDT, AND ME

The Analytic Philosophers Do Ethics at Hamburger Hamlet   56
Doctrine of the Letter "W"   57
Love Song to Fred Phelps   58
Nude at a Watering Trough   59
Rouault's Wounded Clown   60
Derrida, Rembrandt, and Me   61
Wasn't I Eager Enough?   62
Why the Beatles Crossed the Road   63
Free Verse from the Portuguese   64
Past Lives   65
To Mozart   66
The Tarnation of Faust   67

GAINESVILLE, AFTER THE SEASON

Hospital Nights   70
Exurban Condo, Gainesville, Florida   72
Long Days and Longer Novels   73
Within Reason   74
Gainesville, After the Season   75
119st [sic] Street: Central Florida   76
Tumbling Central   77
"Country Girl" Is Vegan   78
Nature Trail   79
Totem Lizard   80
The Gulf   81
Sea Spouts   82
Earning One's Epitaph   83

Playing Debussy in the Heart of Dixie

Picture Poem

An Acqua Velva slap: class photo,
First Grade, Miss Gragg, 1968.
I must be the endearing lad
in paisley, no more tightly wound
than any other child in that odd country
at the very end of segregation—
when a girl named Pocapane
seemed exotic: bowl haircut, browner skin
than ours, and *Catholic*. Poor little bread.
                                            Even poorer
Tommy Akers, who shat himself
one day and met his social death.
"It could have happened to any of you,"
our teacher insisted—not
that we believed her. Happen to *us*?
"Could have" and "did" were antipodes.
Then where does the sweetness of these eyes
come from? My eyes, Judd Huston's eyes, Steve Wilkie
(now the policeman)'s eyes?
I only know I haven't since looked
so divine. Or common.
One of those to whom things happen.

History of the Early Seventies I

That recording of *Scheherazade*,
Eugene Ormandy, Philadelphia,
houri on cover made to resemble
Barbara Eden of *I Dream of Jeannie*,
was a window out of Birmingham,
where I knew several Jeannies.
I thought them enchanted, believing
they must have enjoyed lives
that soared up to the high E
of the ending, higher than my piano
could reach, in timbre if not in pitch—

before I heard Ravel, before I knew
it was only Major Healy's uniform
that kept me from loving him
instead of Jeannie, however
magical her endowments,
only Darrin's dullness
that made Samantha bewitching,
only David Cassidy's hammy voice
that made lip-synching Susan Dey
seem the foxiest of Partridges.

History of the Early Seventies II

"They say Spain is pretty, though I've never been ..."

Who was Daniel, the man Elton John
called "my brother" and saw waving goodbye?
I already found airports melancholy,
and this song made the sadness harmonize,
C Major made light, as Elton's voice, free
from raucousness or glam for once,
said plainly, "I miss Daniel," risking
derision and bigotry before
those things became less fashionable.
I missed Daniel, too, the way I missed
my sisters (married and moved away),
missed the Beatles, missed the friends
mas simpáticos of my old school.
Yes, Daniel was heading for Spain,
and even under Franco, Spain must
have been romantic; it was certainly
far enough from Birmingham to sound so.
I went nowhere, not even a train-ride
to Cullman on a Pullman for me,
and I was always seeing others'
red tail-lights bound for better worlds.

Daniel, now I've joined you in exile,
now the sky is blue, the air is dry,
and I miss "Daniel" the song,
the early Seventies, my bunk bed
with its little radio and shelf of books.

History of the Early Seventies III

Why was Mama Pajama so upset?
The corrupting influence of "Julio"
is not detailed, but the evidence
is "down by the schoolyard": I dreamed
of finding a Julio in my schoolyard,
and there were only Tims, Pauls, Alans,
and other Davids. Radical priest?
I wondered about the species
he belonged to, the radical Father
who rescues the unjustly jailed,
who feels the singer has the right
to be with Julio down by the schoolyard,
overrules the father who has vowed
to put them "in the house of detention."
How street-smart these people sounded
as Paul Simon sang into my prison.
And the mother loved them, longing
for a reunion, loved them like a rock,
the great rock still standing in my mind
after crumbling beneath me.

Funky Town, First Week of College

Tom Petty's whine was everywhere:
"You DON'T HAVE to LIVE like a refugee!"
We stumbled on boxes, over
drunkards sleeping on the floor
of the "drawing room" to escape
the August heat in their rooms.
The Crimson Tide was going to have
a perfect season, but Tuscaloosa
was dying, and showing its best face,
a Christian grin of booze and lechery.

Bowie's "Heroes" blared at the first party,
where the game room was a dungeon
and Thom Jones, clad in hose and heels, with whip,
led visitors into the hole.
My mind wandered. The floor became a river.
We burned ping pong balls for the green flame.
An enormous roach flew at my face.
The next-day air conditioning drip brought
sun-dried beer and vomit back alive.

Wild Horses

    For James Wright

It is the only house I dream about,
twelve twenty-three Fourth Court West:
the dining room with the arched door,
the piano, the stereo, threshold
of the kitchen, where my mother
mixes dough, makes cobbler pies
in which the dough floats, chewy clouds
in a sea of blackberry or peach.
My brother is twenty and drinking
himself almost to death, but somehow failing:
he minds his manners and makes the Dean's list.
The food is too good, the music is too good.
I am twenty-two and home for summer
from a school where cobbler is unknown.

Today, the sun of July and the aroma
of cobbler have brought about
a happy noon: my mother has been singing,
and my brother uncases
his guitar and tunes with the piano.
I play, he plays, we sing "Wild Horses,"
from *Sticky Fingers* (1971).
We sound almost as bad as Mick and Keith.
Our parents listen, unsure
what this sarcastic country sound
can mean, unsure what we are killing,
wondering what part has come from them,

but glad we are doing it, partly for them,
at least, before we leave them wondering
again where we are galloping alone.

East Jesus

>   For Virginia O. Foscue

That's what the philosophers used to say:
"I'll finish school, then just get shipped
out to East Jesus State to teach forever."
It must be somewhere in Alabama,
this college, in Eastaboga ("community
with discontinued PO"), Mount Olive
(PO and BP station thriving),
Duck Springs ("Named for either Young Duck,
an Indian living in the area,
according to the Cherokee Roll
of eighteen thirty-five, or wild ducks
that fed at the nearby streams"), Piper
("Dead town with discontinued PO"),
Sardis ("Probably named for the ancient
capital of Lydia in Asia Minor"),
or Jay Villa ("Named for the house
owned by Andrew Jay, a Baptist minister
and state legislator").
                    Notice
no place is named after Jesus
himself, no south or north, no east or west,
no coordinates containing him.
These are instead his haunts, for he loves
the discontinued and discontinuous,
even the non sequitur—Young Duck
and the wild ducks feeding near his spring
are near his Sacred Harp. Or Heart. He

will eat shrimp in Citronelle, hushpuppies
at the Captain D's in Cullman; he
blesses the blast furnaces of Bessemer.

Smack-Down

A February cold, and on the phone
the strained voice of my mother:
"Have you ever tried to *live* with your father?"

No answer's needed. Sinequan,
Xanax, lithium, Klonopin, Wild Turkey:
They are his children, too.

Half-deaf and staggering he recalls
the bully's blow to his ear
some seventy-six years ago,

tears up at the thought of the awaiting
graveyard plot or Rapture from the sky—
God drawing up his own

like a cosmic vacuum-cleaner,
not thinking that what he loved most
and most abused would have to stay

squarely put in Tennessee
and Alabama: the wayward kids,
the farm, the Jack Daniels distillery.

Daddy—no, *father*—you once told me
the key to being happy
was trimming one's toenails faithfully.

You won't stop urging me to marry.

Grief-Skin

My mother thinks she sees me everywhere now:
driving cars, sitting in restaurants,
playing guitar on cable television.

The family discusses nursing homes
while I learn Liszt's "Will O' the Wisp"
or search the paths of a quiet park:
I meet a Filipino named Ernie.

Crows outside. Inside, the knocking of pipes.
Every other word my neighbor screams
is "Motherfucker!" No, only half the syllables.

Why am I writing on my skin?
My mother chews with her mouth open.
She laughs at everything, she
who taught me to laugh carefully.

I sleep two thousand miles away.
My dreams are all of waterfalls
in monumental cities.

Metronome

My father once repaired my heavy
antique metronome, not knowing
even what a metronome was for.
It had fallen from my music
locker, highest on that hallway,
dashed rudely on the hard floor tile.
He got out his tools and worked
for twenty minutes on that sucker.
Then it ticked more reliably than ever,
a little more tightly-wound,
from what sounded like a harder heart.
You know what to expect: my father
survived a heart attack, quintuple bypass,
intestinal blockage, wild atrial
fibrillation, prostate cancer, amputation
below the knee, double pneumonia.
I outgrew the metronome,
had the pulsing in my head.
I used this formula: disco = 120.
It never fails.
My father's under
hospice care, DNR, no CPR,
no loud Code Blue, in accordance
with his wishes, if he has them. He is
closing shop organ by organ, pulling down
the shades, disconnecting the phone,
moving his hands as if to wash them.

Back Home

Start, sit up spiraling
and the black turns gray at the window

Safe, alone in bed
in a suburb

in a brick house on a street
named after a tree

Thirty years old, rapid heartbeat
but no sweat now

no wife, no child, no dog or van
The night light in the hall

belongs to my mother and father
for we are three again

and spring is early for all the trees
the streets are named for

but shooting up each night in bed
is this dark room I carry everywhere

PALMS AT CHRISTMAS

South

When was I no longer a Southerner?
One day I must have walked down Melrose
watching the pink sun sinking
past the blue pyramid roof
of the Pacific Design Center
and forgotten to miss the rain, the green,
the superstition that was great Material
but left us packed into Mabel's Beauty Shop
and Chainsaw Repair from ignorance
something else was possible; I must have wanted
not to hear the yucking jokes about LA
full of lunatics, all sliding fast
to some divinely forecast doom;
wanted not to kill myself with Wild Turkey
because it was the honorable thing to do
while driving highways lined with pickups,
the bumperstickers screaming (more or less)
CITIZENS UNITED FOR
A JOYLESS CHRISTIAN WORLD;
wanted not to find a teaching job
at some little school close by
Forced Labor Creek State Park, Georgia,
where you could drive for days
and never see A Different Light,
where fifty people hate you for any
of fifty stupid reasons—

and if some goon with an assault rifle
drove past the coffee house this evening
to rid this nation of our collective
corrupting influence, I'd be pleased
to see my blood brightening
the gray ghosts of chewing gum squashed
into the quake-cracked pavement
by Santa Monica Boulevard

knowing it was not Montgomery.

    April 1994

Couldn't Let Go of L.A.

   (after Joni Mitchell)

Foggy, gray-blue lust of melancholy,
I must live everywhere to know you,
the canyons, Malibu, the arroyo, WeHo,
see every garden watered by the snow pack,
by the distant Colorado, through sprinklers
spattering the grounds as lush as courts
at Wimbledon before the serving starts

and even in deadly August the hope
of kindness from the cool ocean washing by
and bringing us the yellowtail, the fish
of heaven married to the sticky rice
of flooded earth in market after market,
a breaking in of presence to puzzle Heidegger,
who searched for exiled gods and found
a thing or two but thought the earth abandoned

yet everything is here, everything
comes to us in this good time.

   August 1999

"*Me llamo Bond ... Jaime Bond*"

(The Melrose, 1988)

A four-year-old girl is singing
in *Gelatti per tutti*: "But I still—
haven't found—what I'm lookin' for."
Alen is spraying "Burn your TVs!"
on the walk in front of Aaron's Records,
beside Melrose Discount Carpet.
Soon after, he buys a television
and a camera. He is shooting
a documentary: "David Case,
Portrait of a Space Cadet" and discovering
flamenco. Tutu crashes our party,
paints a naked dancer, throws
"evenings" of his own, promotions
of his Mickey Mao portraits and slides,
shown in a re-done crack house
in Echo Park. He lives beside
a Gnostic named Steve, proud owner
of six-hundred dildos. (Dildoes?)
Solo piedo adios, Señora Zosa sings.
Alen runs red lights where the streets
have no names, thinking about architecture
or passing men. He tells me
I must never fall in love again.

Spleen of Ocean Avenue

Brutal evening sun won't let me look
northwest (the best prospect), so I turn
due south, toward someone moving in Chinese.
"See that woman?" a father asks his son.
"She's letting her body take her
to a very safe and comfortable place."
The wind blows twenty feet too high.

What is the business
of that horizon, suggesting
that nothing lies beyond it?
And for once the street's too quiet
to drown out the surf, the deadly surge
taking the spin off the globe.
Black white-trash poodle, Cyrillic
crossword puzzle, T-shirt reading
CAMBODIA, a rose garden nestled
round the bust of a thankfully long-dead
temperance agitator:
Santa Monica has come to this.

The magnate and the trophy wife
draw near, holding hands in perfect faith.
From the woman's face, some thirty years

are missing

The Great Williams

William Carlos Williams, despite
his reputation, was a tortured
young man, and sometimes full of shit.
His explanation of homosexuality
talks about "tail-ends" of New England families,
feminized men with "emotional wits"
as out of place in "pushing young America"
as a Tibetan would be.

Here in Santa Monica,
of course, quite a few Tibetans
are walking around. Indeed, there are
quite a few gay Tibetans walking around
and they are hardly out of place. Some of them
are pushing avidly for grades, jobs,
Audi's, boyfriends, rent-controlled apartments.
Where are the exemplars of what Williams calls
"the bastard aristocracy"? The "long, thin men"?
I myself am long and thin, and I may be,
as Proust called us, "*orientale, musicale,
et medisante*," but I am not
representative. These young dudes
belong in health clubs, not in New England
sitting rooms; they have ridden out
their emotions. They will do what it takes.

You Don't Know What Love Is

I remember Palms—fake-
stucco apartments near the freeway,
the dullest part of Los Angeles
and terminus of the longest, dullest
route on a Big Blue Bus—a whole
hour back from school. I'd try
to read, study the sidewalks, study
the other riders to stay awake.
                                One
afternoon, wiped out from teaching
or from a grad school seminar
(Later Victorian Prose? "Burn with
a hard, gem-like flame," oh yeah—then
the man takes Tea!) I saw a guy
about my age, a little older maybe.
He could have been Hispanic, Pakistani,
Egyptian; it wasn't clear. He was
looking, unembarrassed too, at me.
I forgot Pater and my students.
My mind followed my eyes, and my body
my mind, not in lust exactly, but
something still more magnetic.

The Number 12 turned onto
Palms Boulevard. It passed
Overland, then Motor, and my heart sped.
I pulled the cord. Our eyes still locked,

I walked off, remembering that I
had to finish *Gaston de la Tour*
before grading some papers,
but I was woozy, shaking, wondering.

I heard the bus start its slow vroom
but over it I heard a cry. I
turned to see the man leaning
out his window, mouth open, hand extended.
His face was the picture of horror.

Palms at Christmas

Finding it's Sirius, not Halley's comet,
we are humbled, like children being told
the airplane overhead isn't Santa's sleigh
making the rounds. But there is snow far off
upon Mount Baldy—we saw it from the ramp
today, for winds had whipped the chocolate
haze out of the sky, and tall yellow ginkgoes
in strong relief against a wall suddenly
transfixed us. Our first Noel this season
couldn't be clearer than this night at hand
when cold belies what scoundrels always say
about Los Angeles, and young man's fancy
turns to firewood even here in Palms,
ghetto of gardens, sanctuary, and keep.

    December 12, 1985

Auld Lang Syne

KUSC, New Year's Day: *La Création
du Monde*. Milhaud makes the world
sound as ugly as it most often is
right from the start. All I want,
Daniel, is a sleep in which
I can remember you: Why do I
feel your body, rich, deliriant,
several revolving years away
when I drained the cup only hours
ago? "Happy New Year," you whispered
as everything arrived, knowing
the separation would be all the sharper.

January 1, 2003

Fear No More

Virginia Woolf has Mrs. Dalloway stop
outside the bookshop window, seeing
Cymbeline left open to Act IV,
Scene ii, reminding the dead
of their great fortune and advantages:
"Fear no more the heat o' th' sun,
Nor the Furious winter's rages."
Does Clarissa believe it, even in London?
So much harder, then, in Pasadena
of Pet Metropolis, Cheesecake Factory,
the Huntington's Shakespeare Garden.
Still, I tell you, Cloten, *fear no more*
the mournful clouds of waste rose petals
kicked up the second of January.

From the Center of the Universe

South Lake Avenue in Pasadena
on Friday in the evening fog
is the epicenter, Cal Tech's seismographs
waiting to etch the magnitude
of some convulsion. Some say the world
will end in smog. I hold with those
who favor flood, like Byron finishing
Childe Harold, mourning Shelley
lost in the surf off Malibu, for now
my hands are shaking
and my mind reverts to former centers
of the universe, like Athens, Georgia,
or Lansing, Michigan, one day when
the sun stood overparked, as at Jericho.

Here, neither Bible nor *Das Kapital*
can harm me, though who knows what
the Eminem spewing through the windows
of this red TransAm portends.
In the listening booths of Tower,
I evaporate in songs without words,
the muted turbulence of jets, freeways,
and helicopters humming in my bones.

Jesus of San Gabriel

Wie freudig ist mein Herz!

A student writes about smoking weed
with Jesús, his friend: he has left off
the accent mark. An older woman
takes quick offense, saying nothing.
She fumes, walks out at break,
later writing "All non-Christians
should be expelled from the U. S.
because this country was founded
back when King James wrote the bible."

Academic: Jesus, Heh-Seuss,
in a Xeroxed essay, is a simple name,
arresting, shocking in the worst way:
Jesus is alive again, best bud,
God-Dawg, the kid from Nazareth
or San Gabriel who makes friends
unwisely, for friends mean mis-
understanding, betrayal, prison.
Still, we see it works both ways.
When we see Jesus, we see trouble.
We know we will always want that high.

Just What I Needed

After James Baldwin and the Cars

Let's call it psychic retrofitting: Xanax,
Klonopin, Nefazodone,
Propranolol, fortified vitamins,
Campari-and-soda, pinot grigio,
fish oil, Invega, Southern Comfort
(all, as Baldwin's Sonny shouted, "to
keep from shaking to pieces").
In the piano bar, I considered
the interactions.
                      I realized
I needed *someone to feed*—and ordered
dinner for the bartender, whom everyone
"adored," who was the target
of inane jokes about the Japanese,
the Koreans, and the Chinese. (He
was Vietnamese and was soon
to appear in "Tropic Thunder.")
                              But it was I
who said the meanest thing of all the night
he proved his mastery of the Shakespeare
sonnets, his generosity, his
excellent taste in music, his skills
in Method Acting, his ability
to recite his own work well. He
was desperate, he was falling to pieces,
he asked to come home with me, and I
was scared. *I need you to remain
the person who pours drinks for me.*

Sounds and Aromas Revolving in Evening Air

Bowie sings of Joe the Camel, who went
to a bar, but the car alarm plays in A-flat,
siren leaping a perfect sixth outside
the liquor store iron screen

Another answers distantly
and another still, like dogs
searching each other out in the dusk
of June in Alabama

Sirens, helicopters, gunshots, car alarms
build to some last chord, and I dream
of my sweet boyfriend, caressing me:
only his stupidity is gone

Mass Transit

This pen is lovelier than any poem
I will ever write, its blue
the blue of Mobil station signs
at night—especially one
at Sepulveda and Santa Monica,
where I'd sometimes wait for the RTD
brown bus to carry me to Santa Monica
and Fairfax, standing half the way
holding awkwardly to greasy metal bars,
sometimes seeing Leonardo my old love
whom I'd talk to in abject Spanish
(the day we met at the Westwood stop,
our eyes locked in, our hands encroached,
our legs pressed together on the gum-marked seats;
I taught him to say "Hayworth"),
the horde of laborers transferring
at Century City, Wilshire, La Cienega
to finish their two hour ride back
to East Hollywood or Echo Park
from the mansions of the vulgar rich—
and The Eagle's being right there,
20 feet away when getting off
at Fairfax, the Eagle, sometimes rife
with borderline prostitutes, the Eagle
of the red-light-lit Men's room,
of the dark pinball room where I met Ramez
the royalist Egyptian doctor

who liked saying "Never turn down sex
or coffee," and pulled down my zipper straightaway
and smiled a boyish smile at me,
in that order, a drunken tree-trimmer
named Ramon, my first Ramon,
who bridled at the term "Mexican breakfast"
after bucking me for unfamiliar hours—
all stupidly unsafe, unsafe, but lovely

Pavillon des maladies mortelles

Canal St. Martin

I can't remember if I ever saw
a boat, even in the day,
but I hardly ever went there in the day.
Many nights. Below the street—
there was a Burger King nearby,
across Jaurès—down barely-lit stone steps,
you'd go to walk the banks, or
swing yourself along a fence to get
beneath the bridge. The rest is hardly
edifying. I recall
the moans of a bearded African
when I sucked his nipples in February;
clumps of men and flashes of buttocks;
singing parts of the Fauré *Requiem*
with one curious young man,
a lovely Buddhist Colombian
who took me home only to tell me
"I'm tired of living. We are all slaves."
Still, he was vigorous on his old futon.
Toward the annihilation of desire,
there is just one straight path.

Epistemology of Vanished Currencies

It had never crossed my mind, really,
to be kissed by the Seine (I mean *near*
the Seine) by you, Jean-Luc, but it did seem
romantic until one of the tourists'
dinner boats trained its lights on us,
perhaps causing someone from Delaware
to choke on his *aspérges* (much as once
by the Black Warrior River, we two—well, enough.
I say "we" because your name escapes me).

Now Jean-Luc had a lover, and he told me
the lover was just a roommate.
I was one of their pawns, as well as
a sparring partner in long conversations
about *Le Grand Siècle* and beyond.
Schubert, yes; Brahms, never: that's good taste.
I loved to see you laying down the law.

A bed-trick was involved: I now see
that you had me over that night to rattle
your husband. "L'américain!" Pierre muttered
after banging on the door and rushing in
and out. I got pissed and walked out
into Belleville, Rue Henri Feulard,
at 6:00 a.m., the faubourg dreary, reaching
the elevated Metro, boarding, stopping
at Jaurès, Stalingrad, then La Chapelle, mine.

Two strung-out lovers had barfed on the floor.
The train was a portrait of misery.

The first Gulf War was followed closely
in my largely Arab neighborhood,
with its view of Sacré Coeur and
its hanging heads of slaughtered goats.
SADDAM REND SA REDDITION,
said that morning's *Libération*. Let's
leave gloating to *Le Figaro*.
By the time I left, Jean-Luc and I
were on nodding terms in public.
I believe I owe him 300 francs,
which luckily no longer exist.

As the World Turns

Someone is playing (and maybe overpedaling)
"The Poet Speaks," the very last
Of Schumann's *Scenes from Childhood*,
A heartbreaker, a quiet piece
Not too much like most childhoods
I've seen over my twenty-nine years
Come to think of it, but that's Schumann
And German High Romanticism for you.
Still, how seductive the turns and falls
Of this dream song, especially today
When they seem the one refuge
In a neighborhood of Arab markets
In a city on heightened alert
For bombings at the embassies

And televisions half-gleefully
Report the sorties and reprisals
To reprisals much more like childhood
Than any of this music—
But let the poet go on speaking.
Let's hear everything he doesn't have
To say that will console his people
While in the background rise and fall
The rattlings of the Metro tracks
Like the rhythms of the surf.

D---------
15, rue des Ursins
75004 Paris

Little things you said: among them
"Don't you think it was Providence we met?"

And in such compelling places.
The Île de la Cite always did compel me.

Angel, you tempted me onto the roof
Of the Pantheon, where my vertigo

Revived, scar of an old acid trip;
You restored me in St. Étienne du Mont.

You tried to teach me patience, you tried
To set me at ease in vast, gloomy places.

Your purity made me feel like shit.
It made me cry, the way you embodied love.

You said to me *Installes-toi*
Near the icon and the candle.

Once I heard you of an evening
Sing an *alleluia* so devoutly

I could think: of little else for days.
Can that be reduced to sublimation?

Il jaut être vrai, you told me,
But I couldn't tell you where

I spent my other evenings:
It would have been too honest for me

To admit that I passed over or under
The river from you to the swamp

And offices older than Vespers.
How do I know your face would not have frozen?

And it was your face, alert and good,
Not good and stupid, benevolent

Beyond my understanding,
That threw me—a face alert and good.

The truth is not the sort of thing …
Poète, et non honnête homme.

Swing

1.
It was a little rusted, lurched
in its concrete fixings at the end
of each impulsion—
                    we were flying
toward the ends of the pecan tree limbs
over the fence of our neighbor
(whose daughters were, to quote
our oldest sister, "so lazy that
if breathing weren't automatic
they'd suffocate"), away from voices
captured on a tape running all Christmas,
their quarrels and silliness, towards heaven.

2.
In Le Swing, on the Rue Vieille du Temple,
it is clear Jean-Luc and I are falling out
on his birthday, a week before Christmas.
A friend and I speak English
to exclude him; we pretend
to translate. He is not amused.
"*Peut-être a plus tard*," he says
not too icily, as we leave for home.
Then: "Sahm-times-yiou-ahr heht ... ful."

    For J.-L. Marchand

A Dream of Absolution

Yesterday night, as you would say,
I dreamed that you and I were talking
as we might in death, cheerfully,
ironically, respectfully.
It was all miraculous:
The hostile "friendly" on your card was gone;
nothing was marred by inquiries
or the terrible anxieties
of my youth. The friends I made
in ignorance cast no shadow,
and my honest doubt lay behind me.

You looked as Jesus might have
looked in middle-age—
an unexpected beard, a hint of fat—
and your eyes shone as they did
after the Easter Vigil of 1989.

Now, in the afternoon, I no longer hear
the beautiful Franglais we spoke
and I see your stern card again.
I sense how close you've grown to Benedict.

July 6, 2009

An American in Paris

Cheese and golden apples are
the staple foods. With the guards on strike,
nothing to do but turn the tube
to *Buffy contre les vampires*
or *Qui vet ganger des millions?*
The French Gideons have left a bible
and the chaplain visits weekly. His
favorite book is Camus's *L'Homme révolté*.

The language you loved has imprisoned you.
You hear it dubbed over *Alerte à Malibu*
or *Ma Sorcière Bien-Aimee*.
Other felons riot when the Saturday night
porn treat fails to screen. *Tant pis*.
Indulgence and punishment, license
and discipline: each calls for the other
through an eternity of loathing.
Hauled into court, you await a new prison,
a new cheese, fruit from a different tree.

Monet by Renoir

The delicacy with which the twists
and curls of your beard are rendered
show the truest love in the artist—
though it's the kind that can raise
your blood pressure in seconds, become
a feud over the very way curls *should*
be rendered on canvas. The inky-black
which stands for your eyes, hair, and cap
somehow speaks of your soul's ingredients:
a thousand niceties, ferocity, a pinch of glamour.
You covered yourself with mists and flowers,
but those tricks of the light were *les causes de guerre*
in your blessed childhood of manifestoes,
"scandals" that now seem virtuous,
and your many convictions: decorum
be damned! The colors on your palate
are almost extinguished under the folds
of your black smock as the artist of light
becomes a dark prince and *al fresco*
reverses into *camera oscura*.

—But the curls strike me again:
they twist and almost touch the fringes
of the crude, spotted drapes.—

In this dark room somewhere in Paris,
I know how little warmth there must be
and how an honest sun-lit garden
must be for you a specter of paradise.

Pavilion des maladies mortelles

Field of the Cloth of Gold, the mummy
"sumptuous and millennial,"
reeking like jacaranda blooms underfoot.
Trumpets sputter for the moment of truth,
Venetian Carnaval in E-flat minor.
I am that simple: black keys, black masque.

In the pavilion of fatal sickness,
everyone is king, it is always August,
we are all hooked up beneath the skin,
chillin' like a villain.
The College of Mortuary Science
has many programs for those born in July.

DERRIDA, REMBRANDT, AND ME

The Analytic Philosophers Do Ethics at Hamburger Hamlet

Whether to shoot the expanding man:
is there a choice?
                      he encroaches
he consumes the oxygen
                              he makes you
the self-torturer, for he is more patient

it is love he chokes you with
he chains you to the wall then defends
the freedom of the will

his face is still
                his fingers freeze like Buddha's.
While his belly grows, your own is shrinking
for the world is narrowing to his eyes

he is innocent and he will strangle you

    For Rogers Albritton

Doctrine of the Letter "W"

Double of "u," double of "v," conjunction
in the language of the Aramæans,
the traversal and the Ishtar Gate:
double of life, *diablo* of life—
the extra, extra letter,
division that multiplies,
the living wound among the scars,
the thing that is another thing
and not the thing it is.
Life and Non-Life. Begotten,
not made. Library card
for a nonexistent monograph.

Love Song to Fred Phelps

"The Lord works in mysterious ways his wonders to perform."

I thank you for hastening the coming
of the new kingdom, doomed, I'm afraid,
as all kingdoms are, but worth both waiting for
and remembering. I thank you for calling us
continually to God's attention,
for your prayer without ceasing,
pointing to us as surely as Leonardo's
John the Baptist points to something
making its final descent into Tuscany.
I thank you, Fred, for I cannot write your name
without thoughts of the Flintstones and the Mertzes.

Even for wanting us to die, I thank you:
Socrates said only the gods
know which is better, this life or the next,
and I'm sure that what's to come
will be interesting, and that you and I
will not be the worst of enemies
in that blissful Kansas without Topeka.

Nude at a Watering Trough

That episode of *Green Acres*
when Arnold the Pig becomes an artist,
wears a navy blue beret,
and has an exhibit in Chicago
widely praised by the critics:
it gave me hope.
Someone told me, after I'd covered
my bristly scalp with a wide black hat,
I looked like El Greco. Not long ago.
But Alen looked the grimmest, posed
at our bare wooden table
in front of *View of Toledo in a Storm*.
His family descends from the Hittites
and has seen much butchery;
now he works for the United Nations,
flying between cities without electric power.
When Poe ended "The Pit and the Pendulum"
by saying "The French army had entered
Toledo," I thought he was writing Dada.
I have lived long enough
to hear a Catholic praise the Inquisition
the way candidates for office praise police,
the kind that Mayor Daly once turned loose.

Rouault's Wounded Clown

For Lyle Massey

Three clowns without their greasepaint walk
in a landscape meant for King Lear.
No wound is visible, but they step
in fresh-dropped blood, and bloody clouds
hang near the kind of moon that painters
keep in store for times of plague.

Only the dwarf is strong. His
devoutly outstretched arms
and crouching legs support
the taller, long-nosed dunces,
both stricken mortally:
                              it is
nineteen thirty-two, the caption
tells us, and the dull green vest
of the middle clown is the world
between two bleedings. Neither war
changed anything. Man is a wolf to men.

Here are three exceptions. Outcasts
know tenderness. Their tenderness
is great enough to cure, or wound,
the viewer. So much blood. I never
saw wood and canvas stain so well.

December 1, 2002

Derrida, Rembrandt, and Me

The Truth in Painting? No, nothing
so important links us three. It's
something so basic that only idiots
think of it: July Fifteenth, the day
of birth in the dead of summer,
cancer, touchiness, the mother
of all mothers, who must be
reconstructed, ingested on the Feasts
of the Assumption and the Immaculate
Conception, honored in galleries
and palaces at the expense of the remote
and frightful Father—I know you think
atheist, Hollander, Southerner,
but no artist can really be
Protestant, walking with the loutish Luther,
the uncouth Cromwell—those wet blankets
who shut down theaters and shatter icons.
An artist has to travel through the Church
to the mysteries of Plato's pharmacy,
to Pan and Dionysus and Bathsheba.

That day of aftermath, of the long nap,
of birth in the dead of summer.

Wasn't I Eager Enough?

What did you really want, what were you
thinking? Two years later, you remember
a love that wasn't really there, you think
of your own absurdities as "ecstasy."
You mistook eccentricity for character,
wearing colors that made me blush,
a long cord for reading glasses swinging free
around your neck, landing on your stomach.
Dollars for pounds, then pounds for dollars,
but the exchange broke down, even for you,
the political economist, whose
musical opinions always happened
to coincide with those of Penguin
Guides to record collecting. Meanwhile,
the lemons in your water jug soured
day after torrid day, and you never
thought of replacing them, for lemons are dear.
The ugliness of the Tate Modern
appealed to you, the dreary stones
of Southwark Cathedral gave you joy,
as did visits to the ironmonger.

    April 10, 2008

Why the Beatles Crossed the Road

Single file, determinedly, coolly,
they march left to right, disintegrating
in their frozen stride. Whatever message
one is tempted to read ("The sixties are gone!"
"All things must pass!" "The dream is over!")
in this configuration, they are looking
inside, seeing four distinct persons, all
bored by the camera and each other.

Middle of the Road must mean long life,
despite Paul's cancer stick: extraordinary
John, a sulky angel in white, and George
emaciated, already the martyr,
have dropped away, leaving Paul
and Ringo, both in snappy black—
and this photograph, one of thirteen million
set in a London of blue skies and light traffic,
photograph so famous it's more felt than seen.
Yes, the vanishing point is a curving road,
the crack in the S of BEATLES
on the back cover also splitting O
from A in ROAD
                        as a miniskirted woman,
purse swinging, breezes past the holy name.

Free Verse from the Portuguese

> "Of all the barbarous Middle Ages,
> That which is most barbarous is the middle age
> Of man"—Byron

I have waited season to season
for confirmation that I am living,
that I have become truly human,
that I shape and act and am no longer shaped,
but everywhere I see that God
has told me *No, No*: I live
remembering, retracing, in anger
and disquiet, remembering that I
have loved violently and foolishly,
seeing myself diminished without
the violence and foolishness.

Middle-aged faggot! Sucker for the singing
of gaudy middle-aged women!

Yes, my highs now are soprano B's and C's,
I type words of the American
English species, "poems" of no type,
characters of the Punic-Greco-Roman
ilk, gathering a bed of paper
to rest on in the end, some kindling,
a travesty of Dido's farewell,
farewell from the beginning. I'm still
a baby at the point of all change,
veins and tendons suddenly stark
on my talented, tremorous hands.

Past Lives

Drunken at Belshazzar's feast,
I demand that someone scrub off
that Writing on the Wall.

I compliment the Inquisitor
on his fine lace skirts
and his long, painful lashes.

I live exiled in Toulouse
after the Biggest Louis (the Fourteenth)
ices me with *You almost made me wait*.

When I stop playing Chopin's
Nocturne in B, melody all in trills,
the sleeping pug starts howling.

To Mozart

Most art I owe to you, your name
so often thought and spoken
that I don't look at it (though I did at six),
with the puzzlement it deserves: Mozart,
not German, Italian, or French,
harmonizing of the three, I think,
anchored by the slashing zed, between
prophetic opening and guarantee
of supreme mastery, endless making
from the void of 1756
to the more richly echoing void
of 1791, a year
I have always imagined cloaked in black
(yes, before the movie ...) and drizzling
the cold *lachrymae* of early winter—
when you were most wont to rub your hands
with vigor and light the scores with magic fire
music, true magic fire, not the heavy
re-imagining of Wagner,
not the Ode to Joy, but joy, burning joy.

November 9, 2002

The Tarnation of Faust

He read deeply, late into the night,
then remembered what he'd lost.
He dreamed of the woman who dreamed
of the King of Thule, faithful to the end.
He wanted to be that king, and shifted shape,
haunting the rooms of Marguerite.
She would say, "The air is so stuffy!"
She said, "I saw him in a dream,"
when in fact he was there, like a melody
without contours, written for viola
and muted horns. And he invaded.

She loved him, he hoped that he was capable
of loving her. So they sang together
in thirds, sixths, octaves, and tenths,
in motion contrary and parallel,
while the devil in him grew envious.
The child of such a pair must never live,
he thought. It must die by its mother's hand.
When he had indulged his spite, Marguerite
floated up to join her element,
leaving the scholar to his words,
his peculiar fire and brimstone.

GAINESVILLE, AFTER THE SEASON

Hospital Nights

The woman across the hall will not
stop screaming. I'm reassured
that she's been screaming all of her life.

My roommate from Dixie County
won't stop watching *The 700 Club*,
which is celebrating the arrival

of another washed up Nashville singer
in The Fold: after being told he didn't
"have it," he turned to Jesus, oh my soul.

At 1:00 a.m. a trio of Valley Girls
comes in to force a tube through my nose down
to my stomach. I must be cleaner, they say.

Then an angry nurse comes in to draw
more blood from the top of my hand.
She doesn't turn on the light.

The night before, another nurse loomed
over my bed like an angry mother:
"Drink this now, or we'll both be in trouble."

Finally, they're satisfied: I've drunk enough
to soil myself, as people used to say.
Soil, crop, manure. From *souiller*, I guess.

The Christian from Dixie County
is now telling dirty jokes. I have mortgaged
the rest of my life just to lie here.

Exurban Condo, Gainesville, Florida

A slope of golf, the carts restricted
to 19 miles per hour, an eagle sprawled
outside after mistaking the sunroom's glass
for nothing: thus begins the day two weeks
before moving again, the last time two weeks
ago from Los Angeles, which has too much
of everything. I hope that, here, there's just
enough.
       Will I be quiet from now on
in a world of suburban effects?
They are seductive: imagine, an agora
of ten Publix with Fresh Markets next door,
small bookstores somehow surviving
among them, backed by pines almost as tall
as old-growth redwoods—
                      and my head
goes woozy from the insignificance
of every act I thought was critical, good,
bad, romantic, morbid. I've left home (bye-bye),
and evil with it. For evil, one must drive
five miles outside the city limits
in any direction one chooses.

Long Days and Longer Novels

Outside, the frogs and screech owls
are fully downloaded, but the cicadas
have yet to hit the screen, even
in this calm cul-de-sac where a late
spring is changing to immutable,
eternally self-satisfied summer.
Seven-year locusts and humidity
will leave small air-cooled rooms for us,
disgraced as we are in our accounting.
The turn to the novel? No one was
ever more moral than Gide's *Immoralist*,
no one less modern than Virginia
Woolf or Proust: even taken to the movies,
they would not behave, demanding
their wraps and their toddies,
taking forever to settle in,
several ages from stadium seating.
"The Bourbons ruined their blood by marrying
the Medicis!" A backward epiphany
for our narrator, the key to many
puzzling qualities of longer "evenings,"
such as the snow boots, the paintings of Elstir,
the sudden impulse to greet *Mr.* Dalloway,
a type of generosity, the domain of the heart.
It is so dangerous to live there.

Within Reason

Now the house music is mocking me,
women singing like sly children,
espresso machine pushed to the verge
of an explosion. The sky is going south
toward realms of frightful noise and color.
Suddenly I see that Bacchus and Ariadne
(front page, *New York Times* "Arts" section)
are the same person, though Ariadne's
nipples are more erect than those
of Bacchus. Why? His grapey diet?
His stony perm endureth to the end.

Now Game Day for the Gators,
end of all hope for Charleston-Southern,
their high-toned martyrs meeting
their brackish, amphibian enemy
to the roar of devotés from trailers
to freshly slapped-together treeless manors.
The air is heavier than thirty wedding rings.

Gainesville, After the Season

A week after the football has ended,
we are driving at sundown.
I see three people in a laundromat
shaking out their clothes on Friday night,
the dim lights behind an iron lattice

in Kelly's Kwik-Stop; white lights
marking out muted Christmas figures
including a team of reindeer, none
with a red nose ("But do you recall...").

On its mean sports screens,
the Texas Roadhouse has a soccer match
between two teams none of the customers
will ever care about.

A country singer goes "My daddy had a heart
like a nine-ton hammer, / In fact, he mighta
done some time in the slammer."
They serve me a Jamaican Cowboy
without any kick.

My daddy's heart consisted of dark matter.
It broke everybody else's
within a ten-yard radius. On *Jeopardy*,
a bogus tie-in star is sectioning
a cow and stripping the choice cuts.

119ˢᵗ [sic] Street: Central Florida

Peddling ruins as antiques, this town
drives itself into the age by hoping
its pathetic century of antiquity
can by parlayed into capital,
hoping that its swathes of shade
will overwhelm the early August
sun, the disappearance of human beings
from its streets and stores of uncertain purpose.
Even oranges are out of the question.

The once-famous author's house
in Cross Creek, not far away, still
seems the end of the line for civi-
lization, bookshelves showing Gide
(in translation) still defying the menus
near the local churches telling
passersby what the sermons by now
have already expounded. The author,
of course, was a heavy drinker.
The docents of her house offer us
and a local drifter who never wanders far
dixie cups of lemonade with ginger-bread.
How did she stand it all? Visit. You'll see
how easy it is to open your eyes
and realize you're walking in a dream of sorts.

Tumbling Central

The Shell station at this big crossing
is in limbo, the somewhat brighter paint
beneath the old plastic letters reads
(unaccountably) "Shelf"—the business
now collapsed and continental. Ah,
we never knew how much we didn't have,
though we did hear Bowie bellowing
Reh-eh-eh-ehd Money! to end
the brilliant and forgotten album
Lodger. Every DJ has believers now
in some species of swinishness. What happened
to the Developments? The cityscape
is the same, just with the wind knocked out
of it. Are we the new England again?
Am I eating oatmeal at Starbucks?
This summer, all the power grids will fail.

"Country Girl" Is Vegan

So said the waitress at The Top,
explaining the menu to me and Teddy.
(The dish soon arrived, with butter on the side.)
Federer and Nadal were waiting
for the London rain to stop, so we
walked around downtown in a dead heat,
took in the Spanish moss on campus.
Disaster—unspoken but visible—
struck in the bookstore when I
babbled out the first lines of Baudelaire's
"Invitation to Travel," ("to love and to die
in the country that looks like you"). Why'd you
take it so personally? God knows I hate travel,
God knows there is no such country.

Nature Trail

Stay on the high road, or you'll slide
into the alligator sink. Look,
the buzzards are circling,
as eager for disaster as any
millenarian, but the herons skim
across the sinks as if there were
no sudden death. That's sangfroid.
Then there is the bittern at the shore,
sentinel-like, Poe's raven or an honor guard.

Six whooping cranes have just flown in,
straying from the great migration.
Many have turned out to photograph them,
to hear of their apostasy. "They're mixing
with the sandhill cranes, even trying
to mate." They croak like giant frogs
as they suddenly fly just over me.

Though it is late December, I'm sweating,
unable to follow the others. Only
half a mile to the water fountain,
less to the sign announcing THIS IS NOT
A THEME PARK. THESE ANIMALS ARE WILD.
DO NOT APPROACH THEM OR ATTEMPT
TO FEED THEM. How can people not
understand that? This year's crop
of alligators sunning across the water
is the biggest and most rubbery anyone has seen.
Their own children are hiding
in the detergent bubbles in the tangled reeds.

Totem Lizard

I marvel so much can grow from soil
that is only marinated sand.
And what is behind the trees and shrubs
of Florida? An abundance of lizards,
first, and they are close to artists
with their lively eyes (and heads
cocking for better angles: they are
creatures of the Enlightenment).
But what happened to the one hanging
upside down like—well, you know who, the
saint—inside my bedroom window?
Was he caught by the moving sash
on the hot day we moved in?
Living darlings become the dragons
of the dead, so galvanizing that I
find myself on a ride with all
the poets of dead cows and chickens.

I hope that I can find the people
one day, hidden though they are
behind the disused sidewalks where
the ghost of Donald Justice prematurely walks.

The Gulf

This afternoon, it just won't rain, though
we know there's a hurricane
in the Gulf, the water-chasm, off the Redneck
Riviera near Dauphin Island, near Destin,
where three friends and I emerged
one March morning before dawn (after
a midnight resolution to drive
to the beach). How bleak that night was!
Did I really ask to hear Neil Young?
Anyway, "Look Out for My Love" was playing,
with its sinister electric slide
from G to B.
               Today, Moonshine Creek
is dry: I've had nothing to weep over
since your e-mail two weeks ago. No, the sight
of Lou Reed in eyeglasses earlier today
almost brought tears back: *Oh baby, can
I have some spare change ...*
                     The Gulf
in early March, it seemed, might as well
have been the North Sea. I slept on somebody's
hardwood floor, left with that British
unshowered, greasy-haired feeling.
For a long time after, we went nowhere.
No wonder this storm's reluctant to crash
in Pensacola tonight, Mobile the next.

Sea Spouts

We see the funnels snaking
over the ocean—the slate clouds
reverently sucking the malted muck
of the Atlantic by Saint Augustine—
and I am almost bitter over not
being taken up myself
into that very wettest kiss
from the refractory sky
so often slandered on The Weather Channel
where someone recommends
lying in a ditch, covering one's head,
somehow staying tuned to the station.

The spouts are slanting to the south
for beaching, the slender fractal columns fat
and choking with sand and Spanish moss.
Armadillos will meet their Floridian deaths,
but the condos will be evacuated.
"Miraculously, no one was injured."
We head west on a twisting bridge
over the Saint Johns River
onto the straight, flat interstate.

Earning One's Epitaph

It's a documentary now, the lengthened evening,
the sense of time to kill. A kicked-in hearth.
Two songs of pain, two fugues of love, then—
now—who knows what, maybe a monster
truck with wheels like great black doughnuts
barreling down a county highway
in late green light, insects in flower,
coming into town past the Bambi Motel
and CaZabella condos to tell me
that I must come out into the hard light,
that nobody wants my music, my hard-won
irony, my smartly shifting brutal
and delicate touch at the piano,
signature instrument of the damned.
Look at Ian Stewart: he mastered
hard and soft rock, funk and brothel
and gave the world the best muddied chords
in memory to open "Let It Bleed." When
he died sixteen years later, all he got
from the Stones was the near-hidden album credit
Thanks for twenty-five years of boogie-woogie.

About the Poet

David Allen Case was born in Birmingham, Alabama, on July 15, 1961. He earned a B.A. in English from the University of Alabama in 1982 and a Ph.D. in English from UCLA in 1992. Although he lived in Paris for a year and in Los Angeles for more than 20, Case was ultimately a Southerner, spending his final years with his beloved sister, Susan Kirkland, and her husband, Gary, in Florida. David Case died unexpectedly in Gainesville on February 3, 2011, at the age of 49.

www.ingramcontent.com/pod-product-compliance
Lightning Source LLC
Chambersburg PA
CBHW032048290426
44110CB00012B/1003